PENGUIN BOOKS — GREAT IDEAS

Ain't I A Woman?

T0022719

Sojourner Truth

c. 1797–1883

Sojourner Truth

Ain't I A Woman?

PENGUIN BOOKS — GREAT IDEAS

PENGUIN BOOKS

UK | USA | Canada | Ireland | Australia
India | New Zealand | South Africa

Penguin Books is part of the Penguin Random House group
of companies whose addresses can be found at
global.penguinrandomhouse.com.

Some extracts taken from *The Portable Nineteenth-Century African
American Women Writers*, edited by Hollis Robbins and Henry Louis
Gates, Jr, published in Penguin Classics in 2017, and from *Narrative
of Sojourner Truth* published in Penguin Classics in 1998.
This selection published in Penguin Books 2020

001

Set in 11.2/13.75 pt Dante MT Std
Typeset by Jouve (UK), Milton Keynes
Printed and bound in Great Britain by Clays Ltd, Elcograf S.p.A.

A CIP catalogue record for this book
is available from the British Library

ISBN: 978-0-241-47236-1

www.greenpenguin.co.uk

MIX
Paper from
responsible sources
FSC® C018179

Penguin Random House is committed to a
sustainable future for our business, our readers
and our planet. This book is made from Forest
Stewardship Council® certified paper.

Contents

Contents

Contents

Note on the Text

This is a collection of speeches by Sojourner Truth. It also includes speeches and articles by other African-American women who followed her example and campaigned for equal rights for Black women, to show how these ideas developed over the nineteenth century.

Sojourner Truth could not read or write, so we can only access her words through the accounts of other writers. This means that the extra veracity of these speeches cannot be confirmed. This is particularly true of her most famous speech, 'Ain't I a Woman?', delivered at the Women's Rights Convention in Ohio. The first version of the speech, written soon after the event and edited by her friend Marius Robinson, does not include the phrase which has since become famous. The more widely known second account was written by prominent feminist and abolitionist Frances Gage twelve years later, and contains inaccuracies. We have reproduced both here.

Some journalists and activists recorded her words in the southern dialect associated with slaves, which Truth, who grew up speaking Low Dutch in New York State, would not have used. Truth herself seems to have pushed back against this. She kept a clipping from an article in the 1851 issue of the *Kalamazoo Daily Telegraph* in one of her scrapbooks, which said that 'People who report her often exaggerate her expressions, putting in to her mouth the most marked southern dialect, which Sojourner feels is rather taking an unfair advantage of her.' For this reason, where this occurs, we have put the text into standardized English, and in some cases have added paragraph breaks. Of course, this is not necessarily an accurate representation of Truth's style of speaking either. As Truth said in an 1867 speech, 'they can't put things down on paper as we speak, though I speak in an unknown tongue'.

'I am a woman's rights'

Sojourner Truth gave this speech at the Women's Rights Convention in Ohio, 1851. This version of the speech, written soon after the event and edited by her friend Marius Robinson, does not include the phrase which has since become famous.

One of the most unique and interesting speeches of the convention was made by Sojourner Truth, an emancipated slave. It is impossible to transfer it to paper, or convey any adequate idea of the effect it produced upon the audience. Those only can appreciate it who saw her powerful form, her whole-souled, earnest gesture, and listened to her strong and truthful tones. She came forward to the platform and addressing the President said with great simplicity: 'May I say a few words?' Receiving an affirmative answer, she proceeded:

'I want to say a few words about this matter. I am a woman's rights. I have as much muscle as any man, and can do as much work as any man. I have plowed and reaped and husked and chopped and mowed, and can any man do more than that? I have heard much about the sexes being equal. I can carry as much as any man, and can eat as much too, if I can get it. I am as strong as any man that is now.

'As for intellect, all I can say is, if a woman have a pint, and a man a quart – why can't she have her little pint full? You need not be afraid to give us our rights for fear we will take too much, – for we can't take more than our pint'll hold. The poor men seems to be all in confusion, and don't know what to do. Why children, if you have woman's rights, give it to her and you will feel better. You will have your own rights, and they won't be so much trouble.

'I can't read, but I can hear. I have heard the bible and have learned that Eve caused man to sin. Well, if woman upset the world, do give her a chance to set it right side up again. The Lady has spoken about Jesus, how he never spurned woman from him, and she was right. When Lazarus died, Mary and Martha came to him with faith and love and besought him to raise their brother. And Jesus wept and Lazarus came forth. And how came Jesus into the world? Through God who created him and the woman who bore him. Man, where was your part? But the women are coming up blessed be God and a few of the men are coming up with them. But man is in a tight place, the poor slave is on him, woman is coming on him, he is surely between a hawk and a buzzard.'

'And ain't I a woman?'

This more widely known second account of her most famous speech was written by prominent feminist and abolitionist Frances Gage twelve years later, in 1863. Truth had five children, not thirteen.

Well, children, where there is so much racket there must be something out of kilter. I think that 'twixt the negroes of the South and the women at the North, all talking about rights, the white men will be in a fix pretty soon. But what's all this here talking about?

That man over there says that women need to be helped into carriages, and lifted over ditches, and to have the best place everywhere. Nobody ever helps me into carriages, or over mud-puddles, or gives me any best place! And ain't I a woman? Look at me! Look at my arm! I have ploughed and planted, and gathered into barns, and no man could head me! And ain't I a woman? I could work as much and eat as much as a man – when I could get it – and bear the lash as well! And ain't I a woman? I have borne thirteen children, and seen most all sold off to slavery, and when I cried out with my mother's grief, none but Jesus heard me! And ain't I a woman?

Then they talk about this thing in the head; what's this they call it? (Member of audience whispers, 'intellect'.) That's it, honey. What's that got to do with women's rights or negroes' rights? If my cup won't hold but a pint, and yours holds a quart, wouldn't you be mean not to let me have my little half measure full?

Then that little man in black there, he says women can't have as much rights as men, 'cause Christ wasn't a woman! Where did your Christ come from? Where did your Christ come from? From God and a woman! Man had nothing to do with Him.

If the first woman God ever made was strong enough to turn the world upside down all alone, these women together ought to be able to turn it back, and get it right side up again! And now they is asking to do it, the men better let them.

Obliged to you for hearing me, and now old Sojourner ain't got nothing more to say.

'What will become of the poor slaveholder?'

Anti-Slavery Convention in Rochester,
New York State, 1851

'Sojourner Truth', a negro woman, formerly a slave in the State of New York, made some acceptable remarks, in her peculiar manner. This woman, who can neither read nor write, will often speak with an ability which surprises the educated and refined. She possesses a mind of rare power, and often, in the course of her short speeches, will throw out gems of thought. But the truly Christian spirit which pervades all she says, endears her to all who know her.

Though she has suffered all the ills of slavery, she forgives all who have wronged her most freely. She said her home should be open to the man who had held her as a slave, and who had so much wronged her. She would feed him and take care of him if he was hungry and poor.

'O friends,' said she, 'pity the poor slaveholder, and pray for him. It troubles me more than any thing else, what will become of the poor slaveholder, in all his guilt and all his impenitence. God will take care of the poor

5

trampled slave, but where will the slaveholder be when eternity begins?'

Sojourner has attended several of these conventions, for the purpose of selling her most interesting Narrative, and all who become acquainted with her esteem her most highly.

'We'll have our rights; see if we don't'

Fourth National Woman's Rights Convention,
New York, 1853

Sojourner Truth, a tall colored woman, well known in anti-slavery circles, and called the Lybian Sybil, made her appearance on the platform. This was the signal for a fresh outburst from the mob; for at every session every man of them was promptly in his place, at twenty-five cents a head. And this was the one redeeming feature of this mob – it paid all expenses, and left a surplus in the treasury. Sojourner combined in herself, as an individual, the two most hated elements of humanity. She was black, and she was a woman, and all the insults that could be cast upon color and sex were together hurled at her; but there she stood, calm and dignified, a grand, wise woman, who could neither read nor write, and yet with deep insight could penetrate the very soul of the universe about her. As soon as the terrible turmoil was in a measure quelled she said:

'Is it not good for me to come and draw forth a spirit, to see what kind of spirit people are of? I see that some of you have got the spirit of a goose, and some have got the spirit of a snake. I feel at home here. I come to you, citizens of New York, as I suppose you ought to be. I am a citizen of the State of New York; I was born in it, and I was a slave in the State of New York; and now I am a good citizen of this State. I was born here, and I can tell you I feel at home here. I've been looking round and watching things, and I know a little mite 'bout Woman's Rights, too. I come forth to speak 'bout Woman's Rights, and want to throw in my little mite, to keep the scales a-moving. I know that it feels a kind o' hissing and tickling like to see a colored woman get up and tell you about things, and Woman's Rights. We have all been thrown down so low that nobody thought we'd ever get up again; but we have been long enough trodden now; we will come up again, and now I am here.

'I was a-thinking, when I see women contending for their rights, I was a-thinking what a difference there is now, and what there was in old times. I have only a few minutes to speak; but in the old times the kings of the earth would hear a woman. There was a king in the Scriptures; and then it was the kings of the earth would kill a woman if she come into their presence; but Queen Esther come forth, for she was oppressed, and felt there was a great wrong, and she said I will die or I will bring my complaint before the king. Should the king of the United States be greater, or more crueler, or more harder? But the king, he raised up his sceptre and said: "Thy request shall be granted unto thee – to the half of my kingdom will I grant it to thee!" Then he said he would hang Haman on the gallows he had made up

high. But that is not what women come forward to con-
tend. The women want their rights as Esther. She only
wanted to explain her rights. And he was so liberal that
he said, "the half of my kingdom shall be granted to
thee", and he did not wait for her to ask, he was so liberal
with her.

'Now, women do not ask half of a kingdom, but their
rights, and they don't get them. When she comes to
demand them, don't you hear how sons hiss their
mothers like snakes, because they ask for their rights;
and can they ask for anything less? The king ordered
Haman to be hung on the gallows which he prepared
to hang others; but I do not want any man to be killed,
but I am sorry to see them so short-minded. But we'll
have our rights; see if we don't; and you can't stop us
from them; see if you can. You may hiss as much as you
like, but it is coming.

'Women don't get half as much rights as they ought
to; we want more, and we will have it. Jesus says: "What
I say to one, I say to all – watch!" I'm a-watching. God
says: "Honor your father and your mother." Sons and
daughters ought to behave themselves before their
mothers, but they do not. I can see them a-laughing,
and pointing at their mothers up here on the stage.
They hiss when an aged woman comes forth. If
they'd been brought up proper they'd have known
better than hissing like snakes and geese. I'm 'round
watching these things, and I wanted to come up and
say these few things to you, and I'm glad of the hearing you give me. I wanted to tell you a mite about

Woman's Rights, and so I came out and said so. I am sitting among you to watch; and every once and awhile I will come out and tell you what time of night it is.'

'I shall hail you where slaveholders do not come'

Anti-Slavery Celebration in Framingham, Massachusetts, 1854

Sojourner Truth then took the platform, and said she agreed with the last speaker, that the evils of slavery could not be spoken; they could only be *felt*. She felt, while Mr Cluer was describing his treatment in the jail, and telling them that he wife and little girl were not permitted to see him, that he would now be able to appreciate something of the sufferings of her race. It was good that white folks should sometimes feel the prick. (Laughter and cheers.)

God would yet execute his judgments upon the white people for their oppression and cruelty. She had often asked white people why God should have more mercy on Anglo-Saxons than on Africans, but they had never given her any answer; the reason was, they hadn't got it to give. (Laughter.) Why did the white people hate the blacks? Were they not as good as they were brought up? They were a great deal better than the white people had brought them up. (Cheers.) The white people owed the colored race a big debt, and if they paid it all back, they wouldn't have anything left for seed. (Laughter.) All they could do was repent, and have the debt forgiven them.

The colored people had labored and suffered for the white people, their children had been sold to help educate ministers of the gospel; and why did they hate them? If they could not answer that question now, they would have to answer it before God. Even the blood of one man, Abel, did not call from the ground in vain. The promises of Scripture were all for the black people, and God would recompense them for all their sufferings in this world. One day they would meet the poor slave in heaven, 'his robes washed white in the blood of the lamb', coming through much tribulation ('you know who that means,' said Sojourner; 'it don't mean you; white folks don't suffer tribulation; it means the black people, and those friends who have suffered with them') to peace and joy in the kingdom. 'Wait a little longer,' said she, 'and I shall hail you where slaveholders do not come, and where bloodhounds cannot enter.' (Loud applause.)

'What has become of the love
I ought to have for my children?'

Annual Meeting of the Friends of Human Progress,
Michigan, 1856

Sojourner Truth then sang one of her inimitable songs, after which she addressed the meeting in a most effective speech as follows:

'As you were speaking this morning of little children, I was looking round and thinking it was most beautiful. But I have had children and yet never owned one, no never owned one; and of such there's millions – who goes to teach them? Who goes to teach them? You have teachers for your children, but who will teach the poor slave children?

'I want to know what has become of the love I ought to have for my children? I did have love for them but what has become of it, I cannot tell you. I have had two husbands yet I never possessed one of my own. I have had five children and never could take any one of them up and say "my child" or "my children", unless it was when no one could see me.

'I believe in Jesus, and I was forty years a slave, but I did not know how dear to me was my posterity, I was so beclouded and crushed. But how good and wise is God, for if the slaves knowed what their true condition was, it would be more than the mind could bear. While the race is sold of all their rights – what is there on God's footstool to bring them up? Has not God given to all his creatures the same rights? How could I travel and live and speak? If I have'nt got something to bear me up, when I've been robbed of all my affection for my husband and for my children.

'Some years ago there appeared to me a form (here the speaker gave a very graphic description of a vision she had) then I learned that I was a human being. We had been taught that we was a species [of] monkey, baboon, or rang-o-tang, and we believed it – we'd never seen any of these animals. But I believe in the next world. When we gets up yonder we shall have all of them rights restored to us again – all that love what I've lost – all going up to be restored to me again. Oh! how good God is.

'My mother said when we were sold, we must ask God to make our masters good, and I asked who he was. She told me He sit up in the sky. When I was sold I had a severe, hard master, and I was tied up in the barn and whipped. Oh! 'till the blood run down on the floor; and I asked God, why don't you come and relieve me – if I was you, and you was tied up so, I'd do it for you.'

(The speaker continued her remarks for some time, in a very simple and unsophisticated style, and at the close, by suggestion of H. Willis, a collection was taken

up for her benefit, which resulted in a very liberal con-
tribution, and was very gratefully received by her.)

While the collection was being taken up she sang
another song.

The meeting then adjourned until 2 o'clock, P.M.

'I told them I had Bloomers enough when I was in bondage'

This article helped to make Sojourner Truth a national celebrity. Truth had visited Harriet Beecher Stowe's home in Massachusetts in 1853; the article appeared a decade later. In the original, Stowe transcribed Truth's words in a Southern dialect, which has mostly been removed here.

'Well, Sojourner, did you always go by this name?'

'No, indeed! My name was Isabella; but when I left the house of bondage, I left everything behind. I wasn't going to keep nothing of Egypt on me, and so I went to the Lord and asked Him to give me a new name. And the Lord gave me Sojourner, because I was to travel up and down the land, showing the people their sins, and being a sign unto them. Afterwards I told the Lord I wanted another name, 'cause everybody else had two names; and the Lord gave me Truth, because I was to declare the truth to the people.

'Ye see some ladies have given me a white satin banner,' she said, pulling out of her pocket and unfolding a white banner, printed with many texts, such as, 'Proclaim liberty throughout all the land unto all the inhabitants thereof', and others of like nature. 'Well,' she said, 'I journeys round to camp-meetings, and wherever folks is, and I set up my banner, and then I sing, and then folks always comes up round me, and then I preach to 'em. I tell 'em about Jesus, and I tell 'em about the sins of this people. A great many always comes to hear me; and they're right good to me, too, and say they want to hear me again.'

We all thought it likely; and as the company left her, they shook hands with her, and thanked her for her very original sermon; and one of the ministers was overheard to say to another, 'There's more of the gospel in that story than in most sermons.'

[. . .]

'Sojourner, what do you think of Women's Rights?'

'Well, honey, I've been to their meetings, and harked a good deal. They wanted me for to speak. So I got up. Says I, – "Sisters, I ain't clear what you be after. If women want any rights more than they've got, why don't they just *take 'em*, and not be talking about it?" Some of them came round me, and asked why I didn't wear Bloomers. And I told them I had Bloomers enough when I was in bondage. You see,' she said, 'they used to weave what they called nigger-cloth, and each one of us got just such a strip, and had to wear it width-wise. Them that was short got along pretty well, but as for me' – She gave an indescribably droll glance at her long limbs and then at us, and added, – 'Tell *you*, I had enough of Bloomers in them days.'

Sojourner then proceeded to give her views of the relative capacity of the sexes, in her own way.

'S'pose a man's mind holds a quart, and a woman's don't hold but a pint; if her pint is *full*, it's as good as his quart.'

[. . .]

At length, Sojourner, true to her name, departed. She had her mission elsewhere. Where now she is I know not; but she left deep memories behind her.

To these recollections of my own I will add one more anecdote, related by Wendell Phillips.

Speaking of the power of Rachel to move and bear down a whole audience by a few simple words, he said he never knew but one other human being that had that power, and that other was Sojourner Truth. He related a scene of which he was witness. It was at a crowded public meeting in Faneuil Hall, where Frederick Douglas was one of the chief speakers. Douglas had been describing the wrongs of the black race, and as he proceeded, he grew more and more excited, and finally ended by saying that they had no hope of justice from the whites, no possible hope except in their own right arms. It must come to blood; they must fight for themselves, and redeem themselves, or it would never be done.

Sojourner was sitting, tall and dark, on the very front seat, facing the platform; and in the hush of deep feeling, after Douglas sat down, she spoke out in her deep, peculiar voice, heard all over the house,—

'Frederick, *is God dead?*'

The effect was perfectly electrical, and thrilled through the whole house, changing as by a flash the whole feeling of the audience. Not another word she said or needed to say; it was enough.

'Does not God love colored children as well as white children?'

Sunday School convention in Battle Creek, Michigan, 1863

After several speakers had spoken, a clear distinct voice came from the head of the stairs, saying, 'Is there an opportunity now that I might say a few words?' The moderator seemed for a moment as if hesitating to grant the opportunity, as perhaps, he did not know the speaker. Seeing the dilemma of the moderator and speaker, Rev. T. W. Jones rose, addressing the moderator, and said that the speaker was 'Sojourner Truth'. This was enough: five hundred persons were instantly on their feet, prepared to give the most earnest and respectful attention to her who was once but a slave. Had Henry Ward Beecher, or any other such renowned man's name been mentioned, it is doubtful whether it would have produced the electrical effect on the audience that her name did.

She said that the spirit of the Lord had told her to avail herself of the opportunity of speaking to so many children assembled together, of the great sin of prejudice against color.

'Children,' she said, 'who made your skin white? Was it not God? Who made mine black? Was it not the same

God? Am I to blame, therefore, because my skin is black? Does it not cast a reproach on our Maker to despise a part of His children, because He has been pleased to give them a black skin? Indeed, children, it does; and your teachers ought to tell you so, and root up, if possible, the great sin of prejudice against color from your minds. While Sabbath school teachers know of this great sin, and not only do not teach their pupils that it is a sin, but too often indulge in it themselves, can they expect God to bless them or the children?

'Does not God love colored children as well as white children? And did not the same Savior die to save the one as well as the other? If so, white children must know that if they go to Heaven, they must go there without their prejudice against color, for in Heaven black and white are one in the love of Jesus. Now children, remember what Sojourner Truth has told you, and thus get rid of your prejudice, and learn to love colored children that you may be all the children of your Father who is in Heaven.'

This short speech from Sojourner was, perhaps the most telling anti-slavery speech that was ever delivered at Battle Creek, or in Michigan. Scores of eyes were filled with tears, and it seems as if every individual present sanctioned all she said. And how could anyone help it? For surely if there were any present whose heart had failed to beat in sympathy with her remarks, they must be a good distance from the kingdom of heaven, whatever their profession may be.

'God, what ails this constitution?'

Iowa, 1863

The graphic sketch of her by the author of 'Uncle Tom's Cabin' has doubtless been read with interest by thousands. No pen, however, can give an adequate idea of Sojourner Truth. This unlearned African woman, with her deep religious and trustful nature burning in her soul like fire, has a magnetic power over an audience perfectly astounding. I was once present in a religious meeting where some speaker had alluded to the government of the United States, and had uttered sentiments in favor of its Constitution. Sojourner stood, erect and tall, with her white turban on her head, and in a low and subdued tone of voice began by saying:

'Children, I talks to God and God talks to me. I goes out and talks to God in the fields and the woods. [The weevil had destroyed thousands of acres of wheat in the West that year.] This morning I was walking out, and I got over the fence. I saw the wheat a holding up its head, looking very big. I goes up and takes hold of it. You believe it, there was *no* wheat there? I says, God [speaking the name in a voice of reverence peculiar to herself], what *is* the matter with *this* wheat? and he says to me,

"Sojourner, there is a little weasel in it." Now I hears talking about the Constitution and the rights of man. I comes up and I takes hold of this Constitution. It looks *mighty big*, and I feels for *my* rights, but there ain't any there. Then I says, God, what *ails* this Constitution? He says to me, "Sojourner, there is a little *weasel* in it." ' The effect upon the multitude was irresistible.

'We do as much, we eat as much, we want as much'

First annual meeting of the American Equal Rights Association Convention, New York, 1867

Mrs Mott then introduced the venerable Sojourner Truth, who was greeted with loud cheers, after which she said:

'My friends, I am rejoiced that you are glad, but I don't know how you will feel when I get through. I come from another field – the country of the slave. They have got their liberty – so much good luck to have slavery partly destroyed; not entirely. I want it root and branch destroyed. Then we will all be free indeed. I feel that if I have to answer for the deeds done in my body just as much as a man, I have a right to have just as much as a man.

'There is a great stir about colored men getting their rights, but not a word about the colored women; and if colored men get their rights, and not colored women theirs, you see the colored men will be masters over the women, and it will be just as bad as it was before. So I am for keeping the thing going while things are stirring; because if we wait till it is still, it will take a great while to get it going again.

[. . .]

'I want women to have their rights. In the courts
women have no right, no voice; nobody speaks for
them. I wish woman to have her voice there among the
pettifoggers. If it is not a fit place for women it is unfit
for men to be there. I am above eighty years old; it is
about time for me to be going. I have been forty years a
slave and forty years free and would be here forty years
more to have equal rights for all. I suppose I am kept
here because something remains for me to do; I suppose
I am yet to help to break the chain.

'I have done a great deal of work; as much as a man,
but did not get so much pay. I used to work in the field
and bind grain, keeping up with the cradler; but men
doing no more, got twice as much pay; so with the Ger-
man women. They work in the field and do as much
work, but do not get the pay. We do as much, we eat as
much, we want as much. I suppose I am about the only
colored woman that goes about to speak for the rights
of the colored woman. I want to keep the thing stirring,
now that the ice is cracked.

'What we want is a little money. You men know that
you get as much again as women when you write, or for
what you do. When we get our rights we shall not have
to come to you for money, for then we shall have money
enough in our own pockets; and may be you will ask us
for money. But help us now until we get it. It is a good
consolation to know that when we have got this battle
once fought we shall not be coming to you any more.
You have been having our right so long, that you think,

like a slaveholder, that you own us. I know that it is hard for one who has held the reins for so long to give up; it cuts like a knife. It will feel all the better when it closes up again. I have been in Washington about three years, seeing about these colored people. Now colored men have the right to vote; and what I want is to have colored women have the right to vote. There ought to be equal rights now more than ever, since colored people have got their freedom. I am going to talk several times while I am here; so now I will do a little singing. I have not heard any singing since I came here.'

Accordingly, suiting the action to the word, Sojourner sang, 'We are going home.' 'There, children,' said she, 'after singing, we shall rest from all our labors; first do all we have to do here. There I am determined to go, not to stop short of that beautiful place, and I do not mean to stop till I get there, and meet you there too.'

'If men had not taken something that did not belong to them they would not fear'

First annual meeting of the American Equal Rights Association Convention, New York, 1867

Truth refers to two stories from the Bible. In one, Jesus casts seven devils out of Mary Magdalene; in the other, Mary Magdalene is the first person to see Jesus after the resurrection.

Sojourner again addressed the meeting. She said: 'Well, children – I know it is hard for men to give up entirely. They must run in the old track. (Laughter). I was amused how men speaks up for one another. They cannot bear that a woman should say anything about the man, but they will stand here and take up the time in man's cause. But we are going, tremble or no tremble. (Laughter.)

'Men is trying to help us. I know that all – the spirit they have got; and they cannot help us much until some of the spirit is taken out of them that belongs among the women. (Laughter.) Men have got their rights, and women has not got their rights. That is the trouble. When woman gets her rights man will be right. How beautiful that will be. Then it will be peace on earth and good will to men. (Laughter and applause.) But it cannot be that until it be right.

'I am glad that men got here. They have to do it. I know why they edge off, for there is a power they cannot gainsay or resist. It will come. A woman said to me, "Do you think it will come in ten or twenty years?" Yes, it will come quickly. (Applause.) It must come. (Applause.) And now then the waters is troubled and now is the time to step into the pool. There is a great deal now with the minds, and now is the time to start forth.

'I was going to say that it was said to me some time ago that "a woman was not fit to have any rule. Do you want women to rule? They ain't fit. Don't you know that a woman had seven devils in her, and do you suppose that a man should put her to rule in the government?"

'"Seven devils is of no account" – (laughter) – said I, "just behold, the man had a legion." (Loud laughter.) They never thought about that. A man had a legion – (laughter) – and the devils didn't know where to go. That was the trouble. (Laughter and applause.) They asked if they might get among the swine; they thought it was about as good a place as where they came from. (Laughter.) Why didn't the devils ask to go among the sheep? (Laughter.) But no. But that may have been selfish of the devils – (laughter) – and certainly a man has a little touch of that selfishness that don't want to give the women their right. I have been twitted many times about this, and I thought how queer it is that men don't think of that.

'Never mind. Look at the woman after all, the woman when they were cast out, and see how much she loved Jesus, and how she followed, and stood and waited for him. That was the faithfulness of a woman. You cannot find any faith of man like that, go where you will. After those devils had gone out of the man he wanted to follow Jesus. But what did Jesus say? He said: "Better go back and tell what had been done for you!" (Laughter.) He didn't seem as he wanted him to come along right away. (Laughter.) He was to be clean after that. Look at that and look at the woman; what a mighty courage. When Mary stood and looked for Jesus, the man looked and didn't stop long enough to find out whether He was there or not; but when the woman stood there (blessed be God, I think I can see her!) she staid until she knew where He was, and said: "I will carry Him away!" Was woman true? She guarded it. The truth will reign triumphant.

'I want to see, before I leave here – I want to see equality. I want to see women have their rights, and then there will be no more war. All the fighting has been for selfishness. They wanted something more than their own, or to hold something that was not their own; but when we have woman's rights, there is nothing to fight for. I have got all I want, and you have got all you want, and what do you fight for? All the battles that have ever been was for selfishness – for a right that belonged to some one else, or fighting for his own right. The great fight was to keep the rights of the poor colored people. That made a great battle. And now I hope that this will be the last battle that will be in the world. Fighting for rights. And there never will be a fight without it is a fight for rights. See how beautiful it is! It covers the whole ground.

'We ought to have it all finished up now. Let us finish it up so that there be no more fighting. I have faith in God, and there is truth in humanity. Be strong women! blush not! tremble not! I know men will get up and brat, brat, brat, brat (laughter) about something which does not amount to anything except talk. We want to carry the point to one particular thing, and that is woman's rights, for nobody has any business with a right that belongs to her. I can make use of my own right. I want the same use of the same right. Do you want it? Then get it. If men had not taken something that did not belong to them they would not fear. But they tremble! They dodge! (Laughter.)

'We will have nothing owned by anybody. That is the time you will be a man, if you don't get scared before it goes to parties. (Laughter.) I want you to look at it and be men and women. Men speak great lies, and it has made a great sore, but it will soon heal up. For I know when men, good men, discuss sometimes, that they say something or another and then take it half back. You must make a little allowance. I hear them say good enough at first, but then there was a going back a little more like the old times. It is hard for them to get out of it. Now we will help you out, if you want to get out. I want you to keep a good faith and good courage. And I am going round after I get my business settled and get more equality.

'People in the North, I am going round to lecture on human rights. I will shake every place I go to. (Loud laughter and applause.)'

'Women can work. If they can dig up stumps they can vote'

First annual meeting of the American Equal Rights Association Convention, New York, 1867

Sojourner, having deposited her hood and likewise the miraculous bag containing her rations, 'shadows', and other 'traps', came forward good naturedly and said:

'Well, things that past a good while, there's no use over-calling them again. Old things is passed away, and all things are become new. (Applause and laughter.) I was sitting and looking around here – I've been to a great many conventions, a great many meetings in the course of my life-time – in eighty years, and I've heard a great many speeches, but I've heard a great many answers in the anti-slavery meetings. A half dozen would pop up, some pop up here, some there. But in this meeting there has been nobody to pop up. (Laughter and applause.) Nobody to gainsay.

'I haven't seen any one grumbling. I never heard a meeting before but there was great grumbling and muttering going on. (Laughter.) Now, I say we are gaining ground. Haven't you noticed; here is anti-slavery women – a great many kinds; and did you ever behold a meeting and see so many people together – both male and female;

the body of the church full; and every one's countenance looks pleasing, looks pleasant. (Laughter.) It seems to me it's all coming right. Every one feels it's right and good. Why, I've been in meetings and heard men gabble, gabble, gabble; but now it seems to me all pleasant. Why, this war has done a great deal of good, besides doing a great deal of harm. (Laughter.) People seem to feel more for one another. Certainly I never saw so many people together and nobody trying to hurt anybody's feelings. (Applause and laughter.) I guess there's those here that's been to meetings and heard it. Women has been here talking, and throwing out arrows – there was nobody getting mad, or if they was they didn't let us know it. (Laughter.)

'Well, Sojourner has lived on through all the scenes that have taken place these forty years in the anti-slavery cause, and I have plead with all the force I had that the day might come that the colored people might own their soul and body. Well, the day has come, although it came through blood. It makes no difference how it came – it did come. (Applause.) I am sorry it came in that way. We are now trying for liberty that requires no blood – that women shall have their rights – not rights from you. Give them what belongs to them; they ask it kindly too. (Laughter.) I ask it kindly.

'Now, I want it done very quick. It can be done in a few years. How good it would be. I would like to go up to the polls myself. (Laughter.) I own a little house in Battle Creek, Michigan. Well, every year I got a tax to pay. Taxes, you see, be taxes. Well, a road tax sounds large. Road tax, school tax, and all these things.

'Well, there was women there had a house as well as I. They taxed them to build a road, and they went on the road and worked. It took 'em a good while to get a stump up. (Laughter.) Now, that shows that women can work. If they can dig up stumps they can vote. (Laughter.) It is easier to vote than dig stumps. (Laughter.) It doesn't seen hard work to vote, though I have seen some men that had a hard time of it. (Laughter.) But I believe that when women can vote there won't be so many men that have a rough time getting to the polls. (Great laughter.) There is danger of their life sometimes. I guess many have seen it in this city.

'I have lived fourteen years in this city. I don't want to take up time, but I calculate to live. Now if you want me to get out of the world, you had better get the women voting soon. (Laughter.) I shan't go 'till I can do that. I think it will come along pretty soon. (Laughter.) Now I think I will sing a little bit. I sung the other night, and my singing – well, they can't put things down on paper as we speak, though I speak in an unknown tongue. (Laughter.) Now, what I sing they ain't got it in the right way – not in the way I meant it. I am a kind of poet – what do you call it that makes poetry? I can't read it, but I can make it.

'You see I have sung in the anti-slavery meetings and in the religious meetings. Well, they didn't call anti-slavery religious, and so I didn't call my song an anti-slavery song – called it religious, so I could make it answer for both. (Great laughter.) Now I want the editors to put it down right. I heard it read from the paper, but it don't sound as if they had it right.'

Sojourner then sang her song.

'I must sojourn once to the ballot-box before I die'

Final meeting of the American Equal Rights Association, New York, 1869

To the Editor of the World: – We have had the pleasure of entertaining Mrs Stowe's 'Lybian Sybil' at our home for the last week, and can bear our testimony to the marvelous wisdom and goodness of this remarkable woman. She was a slave in this State for forty years, and has devoted forty years of freedom to the best interests of her race. Though eighty years of age, she is as active and clear-sighted as ever, and 'understands the whole question of reconstruction, all its "quagmires and pitfalls," as she says, as well as any man does.

The morning after the Equal Rights Convention, as the daily journals one by one made their appearance, turning to the youngsters of the household, she said: 'Children, as there is no school today, will you read Sojourner the reports of the Convention? I want to see whether these young sprigs of the press do me justice. You know, children, I don't read such small stuff as letters, I read men and nations. I can see through a millstone, though I can't see through a spelling-book. What a narrow idea a reading qualification is for a voter! I know and do what is right better than many big men who read. And there's that property qualification! just as bad. As if men and women themselves, who made money, were not of more value than the thing they made. If I were a delegate to the Constitutional Convention I could make suffrage as clear as daylight; but I am afraid these Republicans will "purty, purty" about all manner of small things week out and week in, and never settle this foundation question after all.' Sojourner then gathered up her bag and shawl, and walked into the parlor in a stately manner, and there, surrounded by the children, the papers were duly read and considered.

[. . .]

'Oh,' said some one of larger growth, 'Mr Greeley is busy with tariffs and protective duties. What do you think, Sojourner, of free trade? Do you not think if England and France have more dry-goods than they want that they had better send them to us, and we in turn send them our fruits and flowers and grains; our timber, iron, fish, and ice?'

'Yes, I go for everything free. Let nature, like individuals, make the most of what God has given them, have their neighbors to do the same, and then do all they can to serve each other. There is no use in one man, or one nation, to try to do or be everything. It is a good thing to be dependent on each other for something, it makes us civil and peaceable. But,' said Sojourner, 'where is Theodore Tilton's paper?'

'Oh, the *Independent* is a weekly, it came out before the Convention.'

'But Theodore is not a weekly; why did he not come to the Convention and tell us what he thought?'

'Well, here is his last paper, with a grand editorial', and Sojourner listened to the end with interest.

'That's good,' said she, 'but he don't say woman.'

'Oh, he is talking about sectarianism, not suffrage; the Church, not the State.'

'No matter, the Church wrongs woman as much as the State. "Wives, obey your husbands", is as bad as the common law. "The husband and wife are one, and that one the husband." I am afraid Theodore and Horace are playing bo-peep with their shadows. Did you tell me that Mr Greeley is a delegate to the Constitutional Convention?'

'Yes, and I hope that he will soon wake up to the fact that the Democrats are going ahead of him, and instead of writing articles on 'Democracy run mad', on tariffs and mining interests, it behooves him to be studying what genuine republicanism is, and whether we are to realize it in the Empire State this very year or not.'

'Speaking of shadows,' said Sojourner, 'I wish the *World* to know that when I go among fashionable people in the Church of the Puritans, I do not carry "rations" in my bag; I keep my shadow there. I have good friends enough to give me clothes and rations. I stand on principle, always in one place, so everybody knows where to find Sojourner, and I don't want my shadow even to be dogging about here and there and everywhere, so I keep it in this bag.'

'I think,' said one of the group, 'the press should hereafter speak of you as Mrs Stowe's Lybian Sybil, and not as "old church woman".'

'Oh, child, that's good enough. *The Herald* used to call me "old black nigger", so this sounds respectable. Have you read the *Herald* too, children? Is that born again? Well, we are all walking the right way together. I'll tell you what I'm thinking. My speeches in the Convention read well. I should like to have the substance put together, improved a little, and published in tract form, headed "Sojourner Truth on Suffrage"; for if these timid men, like Greeley, knew that Sojourner was out for "universal suffrage", they would not be so afraid to handle the question. Yes, children, I am going to rouse the people on equality. I must sojourn once to the ballot-box before I die. I hear the ballot-box is a beautiful glass globe, so you can see all the votes as they go in. Now, the first time I vote I'll see if a woman's vote looks any different from the rest – if it makes any stir or commotion. If it don't inside, it need not outside. That good speech of Henry Ward Beecher's made my heart leap for joy; he just hit the nail right on the head when he said you never lost anything by asking everything; if you bait the suffrage-hook with a woman you will certainly catch a black man. There is a great deal in that philosophy, children. Now I must go and take a smoke!' I tell you in confidence, Mr Editor Sojourner smokes!

Yours respectfully,   E. C. S.

P. S. – She says she has been sent into the smoking-car so often she smoked in self-defense – she would rather swallow her own smoke than another's.

'Did Jesus ever say anything against women? Not a word'

Woman Suffrage Bazaar, Boston, 1870

'Sister Sojourner Truth' was in town yesterday and visited the Woman Suffrage Bazaar, where she could not resist the movings of the spirit to say a few words upon her 'great mission', which now is to 'stir up the United States to give the colored people about Washington, and who are largely supported by charity, a tract of land down South, where they can support themselves'. She don't believe in keeping them paupers, and thinks they have earned land enough for white people in past days to be entitled to a small farm apiece themselves.

She says she is going to accomplish her mission in this respect before she dies, and she wants an opportunity to address the people of Boston and to get up petitions to Congress in its favor. She means to 'send tons of paper down to Washington for them spouters to chaw on'. Sojourner believes in women's voting, and thinks the men are very pretentious in denying them the right. Still she thinks there has been a great change for the better in this respect the last few years. She is rather severe on the sterner sex, and asks, by way of capping her argument in favor of her sex: 'Did Jesus ever say anything against women? Not a word. But he did speak awful hard things against the men. You know what they were. And he knew them to be true. But he didn't say nothing 'gainst the women.' And solacing herself with this reflection the old heroine retired to admire the beautiful bouquets in the flower department of the Fair.

'What will such lives as you live do for humanity?'

This article refers to two lectures, both in 1870, one in Boston and one in Providence, Rhode Island

Sojourner Truth's lecture at Franklin Hall, last evening, was in the main an exhortation to all interested in the elevation of the blacks to petition the authorities at Washington for land out West whereon to locate the surplus freedmen, and let them earn their own living, which she argued would be cheaper and better for the government than to care for them in any other way.

Her matter and manner were simply indescribable, often straying far away from the starting point; but each digression was fraught with telling logic, rough humor, or effective sarcasm. She thought she had a work to do, and had considerable faith in what she was accomplishing; but she said to her audience, 'With all your opportunities for reading and writing, you don't take hold and do anything. My God, I wonder what you are in the world for!' She had infinite faith in the influence which the majority had with Congress and believed that whatever they demanded, good or bad, Congress would grant; hence she was working to make majorities.

She leaves the East soon never to return, and goes to Kansas where the Lord had plainly called her by prompting a man whom she had never seen or heard of to invite her and pay her expenses. Her enthusiasm over the prospect was unbounded, and she said that, like the New Jerusalem, if she didn't find the West all she had expected, she would have a good time thinking about it. A good deal of sound orthodox theology was mingled with her discourse, as well as a description of her visit to the White House, and the reformation she effected in the Washington horse-car system. The whole was followed by a valedictory song in true plantation style. A large and interested audience was present to get the benefit of her remarks.

Her views on the question of woman's dress and the prevailing fashions are interesting. They are substantially these: 'I'm awful hard on dress, you know. Women, you forget that you are the mothers of creation; you forget your sons were cut off like grass by the war, and the land was covered with their blood; you rig yourselves up in panniers and Grecian-bend backs and flummeries; yes, and mothers and gray-haired grandmothers wear high-heeled shoes and humps on their heads, and put them on their babies, and stuff them out so that they keel over when the wind blows. O mothers, I'm ashamed of ye! What will such lives as you live do for humanity? When I saw them women on the stage at the Woman's Suffrage Convention, the other day, I thought, What kind of reformers be you, with goosewings on your heads, as if you were going to fly, and dressed in such ridiculous fashion, talking about reform and women's rights? Appears to me, you had better reform yourselves first. But Sojourner is an old body, and will soon get out of this world into another, and wants to say when she gets there, Lord, I have done my duty, I have told the whole truth and kept nothing back.'

'I can't read a book, but I can read the people'

'Commemoration of the Eighth Anniversary of Negro Freedom in the United States', Boston, 1871

'Well, children, I'm glad to see so many together. If I am eighty-three years old, I only count my age from the time that I was emancipated. Then I began to live. God is a-fulfilling, and my lost time that I lost being a slave was made up. When I was a slave I hated the white people. My mother said to me when I was to be sold from her, "I want to tell you these things that you will always know that I have told you, for there will be a great many things told you after I start out of this life into the world to come." And I say this to you all, for here is a great many people, that when I step out of this existence, that you will know what you heard old Sojourner Truth tell you.

[. . .]

'When we were sold, I did what my mother told me; I said, O God, my mother told me if I asked you to make my master and mistress good, you'd do it, and they didn't get good. (Laughter.) Why, says I, God, maybe you can't do it. Kill them. (Laughter and applause.) I didn't think he could make them good. That was the idea I had. After I made such wishes my conscience burned me. Then I would say, O God, don't be mad. My master makes me wicked; and I often thought how people can do such abominable wicked things and their conscience not burn them. Now I only made wishes. I used to tell God this – I would say, Now, God, if I was you, and you was me (laughter), and you wanted any help I'd help you; – why don't you help me? (Laughter and applause.) Well, you see I was in want, and I felt that there was no help. I know what it is to be taken in the barn and tied up and the blood drawn out of your bare back, and I tell you it would make you think about God. Yes, and then I felt, O God, if I was you and you felt like I do, and asked me for help I would help you – now why won't you help me?

'Truly I don't know but God has helped me. But I got no good master until the last time I was sold, and then I found one and his name was Jesus. Oh, I tell you, didn't I find a good master when I used to feel so bad, when I used to say, O God, how can I live? I'm sorely oppressed both within and without. When God gave me that master he healed all the wounds up. My soul rejoiced. I used to hate the white people so, and I tell you when the love came in me I had so much love I didn't know what to love. Then the white people came, and I thought that love was too good for them. Then I said, Yes, God, I'll love everybody and the white people too. Ever since that, that love has continued and kept me among the white people. Well, emancipation came; we all know;

can't stop to go through the whole. I go for agitating. But I believe there are works belong with agitating, too. Only think of it! Ain't it wonderful that God give love enough to the Ethiopians to love you?

'Now, here is the question that I am here tonight to say. I been to Washington, and I find out this, that the colored people that are in Washington living on the government, that the United States ought to give them land and move them on it. They are living on the government, and there is people taking care of them costing you so much, and it don't benefit them at all. It degrades them worse and worse. Therefore I say that these people, take and put them in the West where you can enrich them. I know the good people in the South can't take care of the negroes as they ought to, cause the rebels won't let them. How much better will it be for to take them colored people and give them land? We've ain't land enough for a home, and it would be a benefit for you all and God would bless the whole of you for doing it. They say, Let them take care of themselves. Why, you've taken that all away from them. Ain't got nothing left. Get these colored people out of Washington off of the government, and get the old people out and build them homes in the West, where they can feed themselves, and they would soon be able to be a people among you. That is my commission. Now agitate them people and put them there; learn them to read one part of the time and learn them to work the other part of the time.'

(At this moment a member in the audience arose and

left, greatly to the disturbance of the lady, who could with difficulty make herself heard.)

'I'll hold on a while,' she said. 'Whoever is a-going let him go. When you tell about work here, then you have to scud. (Laughter and applause.) I tell you I can't read a book, but I can read the people. (Applause) I speak these things so that when you have a paper come for you to sign, you can sign it.'

'You take no interest in the colored people'

'Her appearance reminds one vividly of Dinah in "Uncle Tom's Cabin". A white handkerchief was tied closely about her head and she wore spectacles, but this was the only indication of her extreme age. Her voice is strong, has no touch of shrillness, and she walked about as hale and hearty as a person of half her years. She said her object was to arouse attention to the wants of the freedmen. Their condition at Washington was pitiful. No work could be found for them, and their children were growing up in ignorance. She described the treatment they had received during the war, even after they were freed. "The poor creeters were heaped together" with no food but a ration of bread. Children were taken away from their mothers, and when the latter complained, they were thrust into the guard-house. She went among them, and when she told them they were free, they did not understand her.

'After drawing a vivid picture of the sufferings of the freedmen and their unfortunate condition, even at the present time, she said: "You ask me what to do for them? Do you want a poor old creeter who don't know how to read to tell educated people what to do? I give you the hint, and you ought to know what to do. But if you don't, I can tell you. The government has given land to the railroads in the West; can't it do as much for these poor creeters? Let them give them land and an outset, and have teachers learn them to read. Then they can be somebody. That's what I want. You owe it to them, because you took away from them all they earned and made them what they are. You take no interest in the colored people.

' "I was forty years a slave in the State of New York, and was emancipated along with the other colored people of the State. You are the cause of the brutality of these poor creeters. For you're the children of those who enslaved them. That's what I want to say. I wish this hall was full to hear me. I don't want to say anything against Anna Dickinson because she is my friend, but if she come to talk here about a woman you know nothing about [Joan of Arc], and no one knows whether there was such a woman or not, you would fill this place. You want to hear nonsense. I come to tell something which you ought to listen to.

' "You are ready to help the heathen in foreign lands, but don't care for the heathen right about you. I want you to sign petitions to send to Washington. They say there they will do what the people want. The majority rules. If they want anything good they get it. If they want anything not right they get it too. You send these petitions, and those men in Congress will have something to spout about. I been to hear them; could make nothing out of what they said, but if they talk about the colored people I will know what they say. Send a good man with the petitions, one that will not turn the other side out when he gets to Washington. Let the freedmen be emptied out in the West; give them land and an out-set; teach them to read, and then they will be somebody. That's what I want to say." '

'Instead of sending these people to Liberia, why can't they have a colony in the West?'

Florence, Massachusetts, 1871

To the Editor of the Tribune: –

Sir: Seeing an item in your paper about me, I thought I would give you the particulars of what I am trying to do, in hopes that you would print a letter about it and so help on the good cause. I am urging the people to sign petitions to Congress to have a grant of land set apart for the freed people to earn their living on, and not be dependent on the government for their bread. I have had fifty petitions printed at my own expense, and have been urging the people of the Eastern States for the past seven months. I have been crying out in the East, and now an answer comes to me from the West, as you will see from the following letter. The gentleman who writes it I have never seen or heard of before, but the Lord has raised him up to help me. Bless the Lord! I made up my mind last winter, when I saw able men and women taking dry bread from the government to keep from starving, that I would devote myself to the cause of getting land for these people, where they can work and earn their own living in the West, where the land is so plenty. Instead of going home from Washington to take rest, I am traveling around getting it before the people.

Instead of sending these people to Liberia, why can't they have a colony in the West? This is why I am contending so in my old age. It is to teach the people that this colony can just as well be in this country as in Liberia. Everybody says this is a good work, but nobody helps. How glad I will be if you will take hold and give it a good lift. Please help me with these petitions. Yours truly,

Sojourner Truth.

Florence, Mass., Feb. 18, 1871.

P. S. I should have said that the Rev. Gilbert Haven of Boston is kindly aiding me in getting petitions signed, and will receive all petitions signed in Massachusetts and send them to Congress.   S. T.

'Lord, what wilt thou have me to do?'

Orange, New Jersey, 1874

The little company of Friends in Orange held a very interesting meeting yesterday morning in Association Hall, where they were addressed by two noted preachers, one a man, the other a woman, the former white and the latter colored. These were George Truman and Sojourner Truth. The former was the first speaker.

At the conclusion of Mr Truman's address there was a short interval of silent meditation, after which Sojourner Truth, the venerable preacher and missionary, rose to speak. Her tall form was slightly bent with age, and as she faced audience, clad in the simple garb of a Quakeress, she looked like an aged sibyl pleading the cause of her people. At first her voice was somewhat husky, and a few words were scarcely intelligible at the other end of the room, but as she warmed up with her subject all signs of weakness disappeared. She said that she felt that she was called to her work, and that if we are inheritors of the kingdom of God there must be some work that is to be done by us. That was what she had been trying to do for twenty or thirty years. When she was enlightened by God's love and truth she wanted to know, 'Lord, what wilt thou have me to do? Now I want to go to work. Well, it came to me in the antislavery cause. I knew slavery was a curse. I had been a slave and a chattel, and I went to work then. After that there seemed to be a call for me to go to work for the poor and outcast, for they are as poor as any one on God's footstool.' She said she had tried for years to get the government to help her and give the old destitute people, left destitute by the war, and the young growing up in wickedness, a home.

She spoke of the misery and degradation she had seen among the colored people in the South, of the Black Maria full of them driving up to the Washington police court, of their being thrown into jails, and of their children growing up in vice and ignorance, and said that it was a shame and an abomination, and that the people did not know these things simply because they did not see them. She had heard it said that these evils would die out in time, but they would not die out, 'they must be learned out.' God looks down on these things and sees them, and we all ought to feel that the world should be better because we are in it.

She believed in being doers of the word, not hearers only, and in doing something to show we are workers in the vineyard. She lectured four years on this matter, and had got up a petition to Congress to set aside a portion of the public lands in the West, and put buildings thereon for a home for the destitute. People would sign her petition, but they would say that the plan could not be carried out. It was not so, it can be carried out. She said she wished the women of the place would get up a meeting and give her a hearing, as she wanted to tell them things she could not tell the men. The venerable preacher then wandered from sacred to secular matters, stating her opinion that the national government needed the administration of women to become cleaner.

In conclusion she spoke of the aid she had received from General O. O. Howard, and caused her grandson to read a letter written by the general favoring the object she was working for.

'We have planted the vines, they have eaten the fruits of them'

Maria W. Stewart (c. 1803–1879)

Maria Stewart was an indentured servant as a child. When she reached adulthood, she managed to get an education thanks to free Sunday schools. She became an abolitionist and women's rights activist, and was one of the first women in America to lecture publicly to an audience of men and women. Some of her criticisms of free black communities were not well received by her listeners, and must be read in the context of her time.

Boston, 1833

African rights and liberty is a subject that ought to fire the breast of every free man of color in these United States, and excite in his bosom a lively, deep, decided and heart-felt interest. When I cast my eyes on the long list of illustrious names that are enrolled on the bright annals of fame amongst the whites, I turn my eyes within, and ask my thoughts, 'Where are the names of *our* illustrious ones?' It must certainly have been for the want of energy on the part of the free people of color that they have been long willing to bear the yoke of oppression. It must have been the want of ambition and force that has given the whites occasion to say, that our natural abilities are not as good, and our capacities by nature inferior to theirs. They boldly assert, that, did we possess a natural independence of soul, and feel a love for liberty within our breasts, some one of our sable race, long before this, would have testified it, notwithstanding the disadvantages under which we labor. We have made ourselves appear altogether unqualified to speak in our own defence, and are therefore looked upon as objects of pity and commiseration. We have been imposed upon, insulted and derided on every side; and now, if we complain, it is considered as the height of impertinence. We have suffered ourselves to be considered as dastards, cowards, mean, faint-hearted wretches; and on this account, (not because of our complexion), many despise us and would gladly spurn us from their presence.

These things have fired my soul with a holy indignation, and compelled me thus to come forward, and endeavor to turn their attention to knowledge and improvement; for knowledge is power. I would ask, is it blindness of mind, or stupidity of soul, or the want of education, that has caused our men who are 60 or 70 years of age, never to let their voices be heard nor their hands be raised in behalf of their color? Or has it been for the fear of offending the whites? If it has, O ye fearful ones, throw off your fearfulness, and come forth in the name of the Lord, and in the strength of the God of

Justice, and make yourselves useful and active members in society; for they admire a noble and patriotic spirit in others; and should they not admire it in us? If you are men, convince them that you possess the spirit of men; and as your day, so shall your strength be. Have the sons of Africa no souls? Feel they no ambitious desires? Shall the chains of ignorance forever confine them? Shall the insipid appellation of 'clever negroes', or 'good creatures', any longer content them? Where can we find amongst ourselves the man of science, or a philosopher, or an able statesman, or a counselor at law? Show me our fearless and brave, our noble and gallant ones. Where are our lecturers on natural history, and our critics in useful knowledge? There may be a few such men amongst us, but they are rare. It is true, our fathers bled and died in the revolutionary war, and others fought bravely under the command of Jackson, in defence of liberty. But where is the man that has distinguished himself in these modern days by acting wholly in the defence of African rights and liberty? There was one, although he sleeps, his memory lives.

I am sensible that there are many highly intelligent gentlemen of color in these United States, in the force of whose arguments, doubtless, I should discover my inferiority; but if they are blest with wit and talent, friends and fortune, why have they not made themselves men of eminence, by striving to take all the reproach that is cast upon the people of color, and in endeavoring to alleviate the woes of their brethren in bondage? Talk, without effort, is nothing; you are abundantly capable, gentlemen, of making yourselves men of distinction; and this gross neglect, on your part, causes my blood to boil within me. Here is the grand cause which hinders the rise and progress of the people of color. It is their want of laudable ambition and requisite courage.

Individuals have been distinguished according to their genius and talents, ever since the first formation of man, and will continue to be whilst the world stands. The different grades rise to honor and respectability as their merits may deserve. History informs us that we sprung from one of the most learned nations of the whole earth – from the seat, if not the parent of science; yes, poor, despised Africa was once the resort of sages and legislators of other nations, was esteemed the school for learning, and the most illustrious men in Greece flocked thither for instruction. But it was our gross sins and abominations that provoked the Almighty to frown thus heavily upon us, and give our glory unto others. Sin and prodigality have caused the downfall of nations, kings and emperors; and were it not that God in wrath remembers mercy, we might indeed despair; but a promise is left us; 'Ethiopia shall again stretch forth her hands unto God.'

But it is of no use for us to boast that we sprung from this learned and enlightened nation, for this day a thick mist of moral gloom hangs over millions of our race. Our condition as a people has been low for hundreds of years, and it will continue to be so, unless, by the true piety and virtue, we strive to regain that which we have lost. White Americans, by their prudence, economy and exertions, have sprung up and become one of the most flourishing nations in the world, distinguished for their knowledge of the arts and sciences, for their polite literature. Whilst our minds are vacant and starving for want of knowledge, theirs are filled to overflowing. Most of our color have been taught to stand in fear of the white man from their earliest infancy, to work as soon as they could walk, and call 'master' before they scarce could lisp the name of mother. Continual fear and laborious servitude have in some degree lessened in us that natural force and energy which belong to man; or else, in defiance of opposition, our men, before this, would have nobly and boldly contended for their rights. But give the man of color an equal opportunity with the white, from the cradle to manhood, and from manhood to the grave, and you would discover the dignified statesman, the man of science, and the philosopher. But there is no such opportunity for the sons of Africa, and I fear that our powerful ones are fully determined that there never shall be. Forbid, ye Powers on High, that it should any longer be said that our men possess no force. O ye sons of Africa, when will your voices be heard in our legislative halls, in defiance of your enemies, contending for equal rights and liberty? How can you, when you reflect from what you have fallen, refrain from crying mightily unto God, to turn away from us the fierceness of his anger, and remember our transgressions against us no more forever? But a God of infinite purity will not regard the prayers of those who hold religion in one hand, and prejudice, sin and pollution in the other; he will not regard the prayers of self-righteousness and hypocrisy. Is it possible, I exclaim, that for the want of knowledge, we have labored for hundreds of years to support others, and been content to receive what they chose to give us in return? Cast your eyes about – look as far as you can see – all, all is owned by the lordly white, except here and there a lowly dwelling which the man of color, midst deprivations, fraud and opposition, has been scarce able to procure. Like King Solomon, who put neither nail nor hammer to the temple, yet received the praise; so also have the white Americans gained themselves a name, like the names of the great men that are in the earth, whilst in reality we have been their principal foundation and support. We have pursued the shadow, they have obtained the substance; we have performed the labor, they have received the profits; we have planted the vines, they have eaten the fruits of them.

[. . .]

It is of no use for us to wait any longer for a generation of well-educated men to arise. We have slumbered and slept too long already; the day is far spent; the night of death approaches; and you have sound sense and good judgement sufficient to begin with, if you feel disposed to make a right use of it. Let every man of color throughout the United States, who possesses the spirit and principles of a man, sign a petition to Congress, to abolish slavery in the District of Columbia, and grant you the rights and privileges of common free citizens;

for if you had had faith as a grain of mustard seed, long before this the mountains of prejudice might have been removed. We are all sensible that the Anti-Slavery Society has taken hold of the arm of our whole population, in order to raise them out of the mire. Now all we have to do is, by a spirit of virtuous ambition to strive to raise ourselves; and I am happy to have it in my power thus publicly to say, that the colored inhabitants of this city, in some respects, are beginning to improve.

[. . .]

It appears to me that America has become like the great city of Babylon, for she has boasted in her heart, – I sit a queen, and am no widow, and shall see no sorrow? She is indeed a seller of slaves and the souls of men; she has made the Africans drunk with the wine of her fornication; she has put them completely beneath her feet, and she means to keep them there; her right hand supports the reins of government, and her left hand the wheel of power, and she is determined not to let go her grasp. But many powerful sons and daughters of Africa will shortly arise, who will put down vice and immorality among us, and declare by Him that sitteth upon the throne, that they will have their rights; and if refused, I am afraid they will spread horror and devastation around. I believe that the oppression of injured Africa has come up before the Majesty of Heaven; and when our cries shall have reached the ears of the Most High, it will be a tremendous day for the people of this land; for strong is the arm of the Lord God Almighty.

Life has almost lost its charms for me; death has lost

its sting and the grave its terrors; and at times I have a strong desire to depart and dwell with Christ, which is far better. Let me entreat my white brethren to awake and save our sons from dissipation, and our daughters from ruin. Lend the hand of assistance to feeble merit, plead the cause of virtue among our sable race; so shall our curses upon you be turned into blessings; and though you should endeavor to drive us from these shores, still we will cling to you the more firmly; nor will we attempt to rise above you: we will presume to be called your equals only.

The unfriendly whites first drove the native American from his much loved home. Then they stole our fathers from their peaceful and quiet dwellings, and brought them hither, and made bond-men and bond-women of them and their little ones; they have obliged our brethren to labor, kept them in utter ignorance, nourished them in vice, and raised them in degradation; and now that we have enriched their soil, and filled their coffers, they say that we are not capable of becoming like white men, and that we never can rise to respectability in this country. They would drive us to a strange land. But before I go, the bayonet shall pierce me through. African rights and liberty is a subject that ought to fire the breast of every free man of color in these United States, and excite in his bosom a lively, deep, decided and heart-felt interest.

'The free operatives of Britain manufacture the material which the slaves have produced'

Sarah Parker Remond (1826–1894)

Sarah Parker Remond was born to a wealthy free black family of abolitionists in Massachusetts. She lectured on abolition and women's rights in the US, Canada, Ireland and Britain. Remond left America for Italy in 1868, and lived there until she died.

International Congress of Charities, Correction and Philanthropy, London, 1862

Amid the din of civil war, and the various and antagonistic interests arising from the internal dissensions now going on in the United States of North America, the negroes and their descendants, whether enslaved or free, desire and need the moral support of Great Britain, in this most important but hopeful hour of their history. They, of all others, have the most at stake; not only material prosperity, but 'life, liberty, and the pursuit of happiness'. Almost simultaneously with the landing of the Pilgrim Fathers in 1620, a slave-ship, a Dutch vessel, with twenty negroes stolen from Africa, entered Chesapeake Bay, and sailed on to Jamestown. Here the twenty negroes were landed, and chattel slavery established in the New World; a sad, sad hour for the African race. These twenty human souls were landed most opportunely. The infant colony was then in a perilous condition; many of the colonists had died from exposure and hardships; many others from incompetency to grapple with their fate. Those who survived had become almost disheartened, when the arrival of the negroes gave new vitality to the enfeebled colony at Virginia, and revived the sinking colonists. The negroes were received as a farmer receives a useful and profitable animal; although, at that time, their services were invaluable. In return for their services, they and their posterity have been doomed to a life of slavery. Then took root chattel slavery, which has produced such physical, mental, and moral degradation upon an unprotected and unoffending race. It has always been exceedingly difficult to ascertain the exact number of slaves in the Southern states; the usual estimate is about four and a half millions. These human chattels are but property in the estimation of slaveholders, and receive by public opinion, established custom, and law, only the protection which is generally given to animals. From the son of a southern slaveholder, Mr. H. R. Helper of North Carolina, we have the number of slaves in the Southern states: –

Alabama	342,844	Brought up	1,321,767
Arkansas	47,100	Louisiana	244,809
Delaware	2,290	Maryland	90,368
Florida	39,310	Mississippi	309,878
Georgia	381,622	Missouri	87,422
Kentucky	210,981	N. Carolina	288,548
Tennessee	239,459	S. Carolina	384,984
Texas	58,161	Virginia	472,528
Carried up	1,321,767	Total	3,200,304

Free Colored Population, South 228,138
Free Colored Population, North 196,116
4,24,254

These human chattels, the property of three hundred
and forty-seven thousand slave-owners, constitute the
basis of the working class of the entire south; in fact, they
are the bone and sinew of all that makes the south pros-
perous, the producers of a large proportion of the material
wealth, and of some of the most important articles of
consumption produced by any working class in the
world. The New Orleans *Delta* gives the following: – 'The
cotton plantations in the south are about eighty thousand, and the aggregate value of their annual product, at
the present prices of cotton (before the civil war), is fully
one hundred and twenty-five millions of dollars. There
are over fifteen thousand tobacco plantations, and their
annual products may be valued at fourteen millions of
dollars. There are two thousand six hundred sugar plantations, and the products of which average annually more
than twelve millions of dollars.' Add to this the domestic

labor of the slaves as household servants, &c., and you have some conception of the material wealth produced by the men and women termed chattels. The bulk of this money goes to the support of the slaveholders and their families; therefore the dependence of slaveholders upon their chattels is complete. Slave labor was first applied to the cultivation of tobacco, and afterward to that of rice; but rice is produced only in a very limited locality; cotton is the great staple and source of prosperity and wealth, the nucleus around which gathers immense interests. Thousands among the commercial, manufacturing, and working classes, on both sides of the Atlantic, are dependent upon cotton for all material prosperity; but the slaves who have produced two-thirds of the cotton do not own themselves; their nominal wives and their children may at any moment be sold. I call them nominal *wives*, because there is no such thing as legal marriage permitted either by custom or law. The free operatives of Britain are, in reality, brought into almost personal relations with slaves during their daily toil. They manufacture the material which the slaves have produced, and although three thousand miles of ocean roll between the producer and the manufacturer and the operatives, they should call to mind the fact, that the cause of all the present internal struggle, now going on between the northern states and the south, the civil war and its attendant evils, have resulted from the attempt to perpetuate negro slavery. In a country like England, where the manufacturer pays in wages alone £11,000,000, and the return from the cotton trade is about £80,000,000 annually – where four millions of the population are almost directly interested – where starvation threatens thousands – it is well that the only remedy which can produce desirable and lasting prosperity should receive the moral support of every class – *emancipation*.

Let no diplomacy of statesmen, no intimidation of slaveholders, no scarcity of cotton, no fear of slave insurrections, prevent the people of Great Britain from maintaining their position as the friend of the oppressed negro, which they deservedly occupied previous to the disastrous civil war. The negro, and the nominally free colored men and women, north and south, of the States, in every hour of their adversity, have ever relied upon the hope that the moral support of Britain would always be with the oppressed. The friends of the negro should recognize the fact, that the process of degradation upon this deeply injured race has been slow and constant, but effective. The real capacities of the negro race have never been thoroughly tested; and until they are placed in a position to be influenced by the civilizing influences which surround freemen, it is really unjust to apply to them the same test, or to expect them to attain the same standard of excellence, as if a fair opportunity had been given to develop their faculties. With all the demoralizing influences by which they are surrounded, they still retain far more of that which is humanizing than their masters. No such acts of cruelty have ever emanated from the victims of slavery in the Southern states as have been again and again practiced by their masters.

'Create something . . . That's the life test at last'

Edmonia Goodelle Highgate (1844–1870)

Edmonia Goodelle Highgate was born in Syracuse, New York, and worked as a teacher in Pennsylvania and Binghamton, before going to teach freedmen in the South. She and her sister Caroline both became pregnant by white men who left them. Edmonia died aged twenty-six after an abortion.

This article was published in 1866.

In the sober light of reason, one is often led to wonder what punishment the great Dealer of justice has in store for that class of persons who have amber-hued opportunities, and never develop in their lives – a purpose – never make themselves felt in their own State, Country, town, village or ward.

Some girls and boys at twenty-two or five, – good-rate, graduate from an academic course, possibly before thirty, from a collegiate course – come out into the earnest, hard-working world of realities, without ever feeling that they have a role to enact. Without realizing that their advantages have made them liable to be the grand starter in some move that could draw thousands with them. Too many males and females, with an ambition equal to Caesar's, or Napoleon's, or Margaret Fuller's, or Frederick Douglass's, never make any thing of themselves. Do not even become energetic tradesmen. Why is it? Some of our elaborately educated young men dash all their energy upon some love-sick penchant for some imperious, handsome-faced, brainless girl, who for want of other avenues, uses efforts at passing cupid darts through their gizzards. Excuse me, 'embryo hearts' I meant. Some of our men that might have been good physicians, lawyers, orators, professors and essayists, have been lost to the higher cause of literature or sacred manhood, by this dashing against Charybdis. Too many friends spoil this, and give abortive developments of their own personal ruin. A rich father has made too many earth-encumbering sons, or useless lady shadows.

All things alternately will be tried by the test of ability, and I would not have it otherwise. It is more than a fancy that many of these people, who have been like good gardens, which contain weeds and nothing else, all their fifty or sixty years of earth – death will have exquisite tantales hereafter in punishment for lost opportunities. A real man or woman makes circumstances and controls them. They be deterred from doing what duty calls them to! Never! They control their destiny and observe every weaker mind within the square of the distance. I find it easier to coalesce with a person who has been guilty of ennui, and whose lives are proof of their repentance, than these good-for-nothing aspirants! Any thing which you young pump-strutters earnestly wish to be, you can be. God gives every key to a sober demander. All that you ought to be, pretty beau-catcher wearer, you can be, if you have to wait till you are thirty-five to attain your goal, and do without Mr Exquisite for your partner in an aimless non-existence. I hate a weak man or woman. I fling them from me as I do half-drowned, clinging cats. Yet no one sooner than I would be a strong friend to one who has determined to reform – to be definitely something.

I don't believe in world-saving – but I do in self-making – No – I am no shining light; but I have a reverence for a real every-inch-man, or a whole woman, who earnestly is a definite something besides a fawning husband – liver and corset lacer, and liver and dier by this eternal 'style'. Come out into the glory of God's world of functions and uses – Create something. Aspire to leave something immortal behind you. That's the life test at last. The monument you leave – I don't mean granite or marble – but something that will stand the corruption of the ages. A principle well developed will in science or ethics – A cause will – An immortal healthy soul. Ah! the gods would any of these! Have I said too much? Is it inelegant? Does it not breathe balm of a thousand flowers? Opopinax, excuse me, – but I never wear perfumed kids, especially when I have to touch wads. Up! work, make something out of yourself, even if it is like getting blood from a turnip. Try! The race needs living, working demonstrations – the world does. Young man, the master in world-reconstruction has called; is calling, but will not enact, for you and your sister.

'Often have I been told if I were a man I would be hung'

Jennie Carter (c. 1830–1881)

Social commentator Jennie Carter's pen names included Semper Fidelis and Ann J. Trask. She was probably born in New Orleans, and moved west to California.

This article was published in 1868.

Mr Editor: – There is in the present political campaign less bitterness than heretofore at the North, while at the South it is increased ten-fold. A Democrat said the other day, that the feeling exhibited South was 'caused by negroes seeking equality, and the people would not endure it and the despotism it brought them'. They can't stand despotism. I think they ought to, for they have dealt largely in that material. Until the rebellion, who dared to express an opinion adverse to human bondage south of Mason and Dixon's line? Who dared read the first clause of the Constitution – 'All men are born free and equal' – and give it a literal interpretation? And who dared preach the whole gospel – that master and servant were equal? Who dared to be seen reading the New

York *Tribune*. All must put a lock on their lips, or suffer imprisonment and death. I know what I write, having spent a great portion of my life there; and often have I been told if I were a man I would be hung: and for what? Why, for saying slavery was wrong.

I recollect one time, in B— country, Kentucky, I sat up all night with a poor slave mother, who lay in spasms, caused by the selling to a negro trader of her little boy, not three years of age. When in the morning her master came to her cabin to see how she was, I began to plead with him in humanity's name; and when that would not move him, I told him God was just, and would not suffer such things forever. He told me I had said enough to hang me.

They had better not talk of despotism and military rule now. I am sure they have more liberty than they ever allowed others. They can all speak their minds fully – even curse the Government that ought to have hung them; and now that we have the blood-bought right to speak of Christianity, humanity, morality and justice, and they cannot muzzle us, they cry 'negro equality!'

We do not desire equality with them. I hope none of us are so low and so lost to all that is noble as to wish to change places with those slave owners (all Democrats), who before the war raised men and women for the market – selling their own flesh and blood, separating husband and wife, parent and child. No, we never expect to be bad enough to be their equals. As regards color, the slave-holders did all they could to produce equality. I know many of them whose daughters in the big house were not as light as their daughters in the cabin. And when I hear the Democrats say, 'Want your daughter to marry a nigger?' I tell them many of your daughters have married negroes, and many more would have done it, but you choose to sell them to white men to become victims of their lust. Shame! I say. I am tired of listening to their falsehoods, and thankful that the Chinese can rest. Last year it was Chinese and Negro; this year not one word about the 'moon-eyed celestials'; and next year they will be patting you on the shoulder, saying, 'Come friend, give us your vote.' Then should every one have the courage to say, 'Depart, I never knew you, ye workers of iniquity.'

'The best way for a man to prove that he can do a thing is to do it'

Fannie Jackson Coppin (1837–1913)

Fannie Jackson Coppin was born a slave in Washington, DC, and orphaned young. Her freedom was purchased by her aunt when she was twelve. She studied at Oberlin College, and worked variously as an educator, a writer and a missionary.

Philadelphia, 1879

The great lesson to be taught by this Fair is the value of co-operative effort to make our cents dollars, and to show us what help there is for ourselves in ourselves. That the colored people of this country have enough money to materially alter their financial condition, was clearly demonstrated by the millions of dollars deposited in the Freedmen's Bank; that they have the good sense, and the unanimity to use this power, are now proved by this industrial exhibition and fair.

It strikes me that much of the recent talk about the exodus has proceeded upon the high-handed assumption that, owing largely to the credit system of the South, the colored people there are forced to the alternative, to 'curse God, and die', or else 'go West'. Not a bit of it. The people of the South, it is true, cannot at this time produce hundreds of dollars, but they have millions of pennies; and millions of pennies make tens of thousands of dollars. By clubbing together and lumping their pennies, a fund might be raised in the cities of the South that the poorer classes might fall back upon while their crops are growing; or else, by the opening of co-operative stores, become their own creditors and so effectually rid themselves of their merciless extortioners. 'Oh, they won't do anything; you can't get them united on anything!' is frequently expressed. The best way for a man to prove that he can do a thing is to do it, and that is what we have shown we can do. This fair, participated in by twenty four States in the Union, and gotten up for a purpose which is of no pecuniary benefit to those concerned in it, effectually silences all slanders about 'we won't or we can't do', and teaches its own instructive and greatly needed lessons of self-help, – the best help that any man can have, next to God's.

Those in charge, who have completed the arrangement of the Fair, have studiously avoided preceding it with noisy and demonstrative babblings, which are so often the vapid precursors of promises as empty as those who make them; therefore, in some quarters, our Fair has been overlooked. It is not, we think, a presumptuous interpretation of this great movement, to say, that the voice of God now seems to utter 'Speak to the people that they go forward.' 'Go forward' in what respect?

Teach the millions of poor colored laborers of the South how much power they have in themselves, by co-operation of effort, and by a combination of their small means, to change the despairing poverty which now drives them from their homes, and makes them a mill-stone around the neck of any community, South or West. Secondly, that we shall go forward in asking to enter the same employments which other people enter. Within the past ten years we have made almost no advance in getting our youth into industrial and business occupations. It is just as hard for instance, to get a boy into a printing-office now as it was ten years ago. It is simply astonishing when we consider how many of the common vocations of life colored people are shut out of. Colored men are not admitted to the printers' trade-union, nor, with very rare exceptions are they employed in any city of the United States in a paid capacity as printers or writers; one of the rare exceptions being the employment of H. Price Williams, on the *Sunday Press* of this city. We are not employed as salesmen or pharmacists, or saleswomen, or bank clerks, or merchants' clerks, or tradesmen, or mechanics, or telegraph operators, or to any degree as State or government officials, and I could keep on with the string of 'ors' until tomorrow morning, but the patience of an audience has its limit.

Slavery made us poor, and its gloomy, malicious shadow tends to keep us so. I beg to say, kind hearers, that this is not spoken in a spirit of recrimination. We have no quarrel with our fate, and we leave your

Christianity to yourselves. Our faith is firmly fixed in that 'Eternal Providence', that in its own good time will 'justify the ways of God to man'. But, believing that to get the right men into the right places is a 'consummation most devoutly to be wished', it is a matter of serious concern to us to see our youth with just as decided diversity of talent as any other people, herded together into but three or four occupations.

It is cruel to make a teacher or a preacher of a man who ought to be a printer or a blacksmith, and that is exactly the condition we are now obliged to submit to. The greatest advance that has been made since the War has been effected by political parties, and it is precisely the political positions that we think it least desirable our youth should fill. We have our choice of the professions, it is true, but, as we have not been endowed with an overwhelming abundance of brains, it is not probable that we can contribute to the bar a great lawyer except once in a great while. The same may be said of medicine; nor are we able to tide over the 'starving time', between the reception of a diploma and the time that a man's profession becomes a paying one.

Being determined to know whether this industrial and business ostracism lay in ourselves or 'in our stars', we have from time to time, knocked, shaken, and kicked, at these closed doors of employment. A cold, metallic voice from within replies, 'We do not employ colored people.' Ours not to make reply, ours not to question why. Thank heaven, we are not obliged to do and die; having the preference to do or die, we naturally prefer to do.

But we cannot help wondering if some ignorant or faithless steward of God's work and God's money hasn't blundered. It seems necessary that we should make known to the good men and women who are so solicitous about our souls, and our minds, that we haven't quite got rid of our bodies yet, and until we do, we must feed and clothe them; and this attitude of keeping us out of work forces us back upon charity.

That distinguished thinker, Mr Henry C. Carey, in his valuable works on political economy, has shown by the truthful and forceful logic of history, that the elevation of all peoples to a higher moral and intellectual plane, and to a fuller investiture of their civil rights, has always steadily kept pace with the improvement in their physical condition. Therefore we feel that resolutely and in unmistakable language, yet in the dignity of moderation, we should strive to make known to all men the justice of our claims to the same employments as other's under the same conditions. We do not ask that anyone of our people shall be put into a position because he is a colored person, but we do most emphatically ask that he shall not be kept out of a position because he is a colored person. 'An open field and no favors' is all that is requested. The time was when to put a colored girl or boy behind a counter would have been to decrease custom; it would have been a tax upon the employer, and a charity that we were too proud to accept; but public sentiment has changed. I am satisfied that the employment of a colored clerk or a colored saleswoman wouldn't even be a 'nine days' wonder'. It is easy of accomplishment, and yet it is not. To thoughtless and headstrong people who meet duty with impertinent dictation I do not now address myself; but to those who wish the most gracious of all blessings, a fuller enlightment as to their duty, – to those I beg to say, think of what is suggested in this appeal.

'We are the heirs of a past which was not our fathers' moulding'

Anna Julia Cooper (1860–1964)

Anna Julia Cooper was born into slavery in North Carolina, but was freed after the Emancipation Proclamation. She began her studies aged nine thanks to a scholarship, and ultimately went on to receive a PhD in History from the University of Paris-Sorbonne.

Protestant Episcopal Church, Washington, DC, 1886

The race is just twenty-one years removed from the conception and experience of a chattel, just at the age of ruddy manhood. It is well enough to pause a moment for retrospection, introspection, and prospection. We look back, not to become inflated with conceit because of the depths from which we have arisen, but that we may learn wisdom from experience. We look within that we may gather together once more our forces, and, by improved and more practical methods, address ourselves to the tasks before us. We look forward with hope and trust that the same God whose guiding hand led our fathers through and out of the gall and bitterness of oppression, will still lead and direct their children, to the honor of His name, and for their ultimate salvation.

But this survey of the failures or achievments of the past, the difficulties and embarrassments of the present, and the mingled hopes and fears for the future, must not degenerate into mere dreaming nor consume the time which belongs to the practical and effective handling of the crucial questions of the hour; and there can be no issue more vital and momentous than this of the womanhood of the race.

Here is the vulnerable point, not in the heel, but at the heart of the young Achilles; and here must the defenses be strengthened and the watch redoubled.

We are the heirs of a past which was not our fathers' moulding. 'Every man the arbiter of his own destiny' was not true for the American Negro of the past: and it is no fault of his that he finds himself today the inheritor of a manhood and womanhood impoverished and debased by two centuries and more of compression and degradation.

But weaknesses and malformations, which today are attributable to a vicious schoolmaster and a pernicious system, will a century hence be rightly regarded as proofs of innate corruptness and radical incurability.

Now the fundamental agency under God in the regeneration, the re-training of the race, as well as the ground work and starting point of its progress upward, must be the *black woman*.

With all the wrongs and neglects of her past, with all

the weakness, the debasement, the moral thralldom of her present, the black woman of today stands mute and wondering at the Herculean task devolving around her. But the cycles wait for her. No other hand can move the lever. She must be loosed from her bands and set to work.

Our meager and superficial results from past efforts prove their futility; and every attempt to elevate the Negro, whether undertaken by himself or through the philanthropy of others, cannot but prove abortive unless so directed as to utilize the indispensable agency of an elevated and trained womanhood.

A race cannot be purified from without. Preachers and teachers are helps, and stimulants and conditions as necessary as the gracious rain and sunshine are to plant growth. But what are rain and dew and sunshine and cloud if there be no life in the plant germ? We must go to the root and see that it is sound and healthy and vigorous; and not deceive ourselves with waxen flowers and painted leaves of mock chlorophyll.

We too often mistake individuals' honor for race development and so are ready to substitute pretty accomplishments for sound sense and earnest purpose.

A stream cannot rise higher than its source. The atmosphere of homes is no rarer and purer and sweeter than are the mothers in those homes. A race is but a total of families. The nation is the aggregate of its homes. As the whole is sum of all its parts, so the character of the parts will determine the characteristics of the whole. These are all axioms and so evident that it seems gratuitous to remark it; and yet, unless I am greatly mistaken, most of the unsatisfaction from our past results arises from just such a radical and palpable error, as much almost on our own part as on that of our benevolent white friends.

The Negro is constitutionally hopeful and proverbially irrepressible; and naturally stands in danger of being dazzled by the shimmer and tinsel of superficials. We often mistake foliage for fruit and overestimate or wrongly estimate brilliant results.

The late Martin R. Delany, who was an unadulterated black man, used to say when honors of state fell upon him, that when he entered the council of kings the black race entered with him; meaning, I suppose, that there was no discounting his race identity and attributing his achievements to some admixture of Saxon blood. But our present record of eminent men, when placed beside the actual status of the race in America today, proves that no man can represent the race. Whatever the attainments of the individual may be, unless his home has moved on *pari passu*, he can never be regarded as identical with or representative of the whole.

Not by pointing to sun-bathed mountain tops do we prove that Phoebus warms the valleys. We must point to homes, average homes, homes of the rank and file of horny handed toiling men and women of the South (where the masses are) lighted and cheered by the good, the beautiful, and the true, – then and not till then will the whole plateau be lifted into the sunlight.

Only the BLACK WOMAN can say 'when and where

I enter, in the quiet, undisputed dignity of my woman-hood, without violence and without suing or special patronage, then and there the whole *Negro race enters with me.*' Is it not evident then that as individual workers for this race we must address ourselves with no half-hearted zeal to this feature of our mission. The need is felt and must be recognized by all. There is a call for workers, for missionaries, for men and women with the double consecration of a fundamental love of humanity and a desire for its melioration through the Gospel; but superadded to this we demand an intelligent and sympathetic comprehension of the interests and special needs of the Negro.

I see not why there should not be an organized effort for the protection and elevation of our girls such as the White Cross League in England. English women are strengthened and protected by more than twelve centuries of Christian influences, freedom and civilization; English girls are dispirited and crushed down by no such all-levelling prejudice as that supercilious caste spirit in America which cynically assumes 'A Negro woman cannot be a lady.' English womanhood is beset by no such snares and traps as betray the unprotected, untrained colored girl of the South, whose only crime and dire destruction often is her unconscious and marvelous beauty. Surely then if English indignation is aroused and English manhood thrilled under the leadership of a Bishop of the English church to build up bulwarks around their wronged sisters, Negro sentiment cannot remain callous and Negro effort nerveless in view of the imminent peril of the mothers of the next generation. *'I am my Sister's keeper!'* should be the hearty response of every man and woman of the race, and this conviction should purify and exalt the narrow, selfish and petty personal aims of life into a noble and sacred purpose.

We need men who can let their interest and gallantry extend outside the circle of their aesthetic appreciation; men who can be a father, a brother, a friend to every weak, struggling unshielded girl. We need women who are so sure of their own social footing that they need not fear leaning to lend a hand to a fallen or falling sister. We need men and women who do not exhaust their genius splitting hairs on aristocratic distinctions and thanking God they are not as others; but earnest, unselfish souls, who can go into the highways and byways, lifting up and leading, advising and encouraging with the truly catholic benevolence of the Gospel of Christ.

'We are women, American women'

Josephine St. Pierre Ruffin (1842–1924)

Josephine St Pierre Ruffin was born into a wealthy Boston family; her father was from Martinique and her mother from England. She was one of the founding members of the American Woman Suffrage Association, the National Federation of Afro-American Women and the NAACP, among other organizations. Ruffin also founded and edited the Woman's Era, *the first American newspaper published by and for African-American women.*

First National Conference of the Colored
Women of America, Boston, 1895

I have left the strongest reason for our conferring together until the last. All over America there is to be found a large and growing class of earnest, intelligent, progressive colored women, women who, if not leading full useful lives, are only waiting for the opportunity to do so, many of them warped and cramped for lack of opportunity, not only to do more but to *be* more; and yet, if an estimate of the colored women of America is called for, the inevitable reply, glibly given is: 'For the most part ignorant and immoral, some exceptions, of course, but these don't count.' Now for the sake of the thousands of self-sacrificing young women teaching and preaching in lonely southern backwoods, for the noble army of mothers who have given birth to these girls, mothers whose intelligence is only limited by their opportunity to get at books, for the sake of the fine cultured women who have carried off the honors in school here and often abroad, for the sake of our own dignity, the dignity of our race and the future good name of our children, it is 'mete, right and our bounded duty' to stand forth and declare ourselves and principles, to teach an ignorant and suspicious world that our aims and interests are identical with those of all good aspiring women.

Too long have we been silent under unjust and unholy charges; we cannot expect to have them removed until we disprove them through ourselves. It is not enough to try and disprove unjust charges through individual effort that never goes any further. Year after year southern women have protested against the admission of colored women into any national organization on the ground of the immorality of these women, and because all refutation has only been tried by individual work the charge has never been crushed, as it could and should have been at the first. Now with an army of organized women standing for purity and mental worth, we in ourselves deny the charge and open the eyes of the world to a state of affairs to which they have been blind, often willfully so, and the very fact that the charges, audaciously and flippantly made, as they often are, are of so humiliating and delicate a nature, serves to protect the accuser by driving the helpless accused into mortified silence. It is to break this silence, not by noisy protestations of what we are not, but by a dignified showing of what we are and hope to become that we are impelled to take this step, to make of this gathering an object lesson to the world.

For many and apparent reasons it is especially fitting that the women of the race take the lead in this movement, but for all this we recognize the necessity of the sympathy of our husbands, brothers and fathers. Our woman's movement is woman's movement in that it is led and directed by women for the good of women and men, for the benefit of all humanity, which is more than any one branch or section of it. We want, we ask the active interest of our men, and, too, we are not drawing the color line; we are women, American women, as intensely interested in all that pertains to us as such as all other American women: we are not alienating or withdrawing, we are only coming to the front, willing to join any others in the same work and cordially inviting and welcoming any others to join us. If there is any one thing I would especially enjoin upon this conference it is union and earnestness. The questions that are to come before us are of too much import to be weakened by any trivialities or personalities. If any differences arise, let them be quickly settled, with the feeling that we are all workers to the same end, to elevate and dignify colored American womanhood.

This conference will not be what I expect if it does not show the wisdom, indeed the absolute necessity of a national organization of our women. Every year new questions coming up will prove it to us. This hurried, almost informal convention does not begin to meet our needs, it is only a beginning, made here in dear old Boston, where the scales of justice and generosity hang evenly balanced, and where the people 'dare be true' to their best instincts and stand ready to lend aid and sympathy to worthy strugglers. It is hoped and believed that from this will spring an organization that will in truth bring in a new era to the colored women of America.

List of Sources

'I am a woman's rights'

> 'Woman's Rights Convention', Salem,
> Ohio, *Anti-Slavery Bugle*, 21 June 1851.

'And ain't I a woman?'

> Frances D. Gage, 'Sojourner Truth',
> *New York Independent*, 23 April 1863.

'What will become of the poor slaveholder?'

> 'Anti-Slavery Convention at Rochester, NY – George
> Thompson', *Liberator*, 4 April 1851.

'We'll have our rights; see if we don't'

> Elizabeth Cady Stanton, Susan B. Anthony and
> Matilda Joslyn Gage, *History of Woman Suffrage*
> (New York: Fowler and Wells, 1881), Vol. 1.

'I shall hail you where slaveholders do not come'

> 'Proceedings at the Anti-Slavery
> Celebration at Framingham,
> July 4, 1854', *Liberator*, 14 July 1854.

List of Sources

*'What has become of the love I ought
to have for my children?'*

'Proceedings of the Annual Meeting
of the Friends of Human Progress in Michigan',
Anti-Slavery Bugle, 8 November 1856.

*'I told them I had Bloomers enough
when I was in bondage'*

Harriet Beecher Stowe, 'Sojourner Truth,
the Libyan Sibyl', *Atlantic Monthly*, April 1863.

*'Does not God love colored children
as well as white children?'*

National Anti-Slavery Standard, 11 July 1863.

'God, what ails this constitution?'

*Narrative of Sojourner Truth; A Bondswoman of
Olden Time, With a History of Her Labors and
Correspondence Drawn from Her 'Book of Life'; Also,
A Memorial Chapter* (Penguin Classics, 1998).

*'We do as much, we eat as much,
we want as much'*

American Equal Rights Association, et al., *Proceed-
ings of the First Anniversary of the American Equal
Rights Association, Held at the Church of the Puritans,
New York, May 9 and 10, 1867* (New York:
Robert J. Johnston, Printer, 1867).

List of Sources

*'If men had not taken something that did not belong
to them they would not fear'*

> 'Address of Sojourner Truth',
> *National Anti-Slavery Standard*, 1 June 1867.

*'Women can work. If they can dig up
stumps they can vote'*

> American Equal Rights Association, et al.,
> *Proceedings of the First Anniversary of the
> American Equal Rights Association,
> Held at the Church of the Puritans,
> New York, May 9 and 10, 1867* (New York:
> Robert J. Johnston, Printer, 1867).

'I must sojourn once to the ballot-box before I die'

> Stanton et al., *History of Woman Suffrage*, Vol. 2.

*'Did Jesus ever say anything against women?
Not a word'*

> *Narrative of Sojourner Truth.*

'What will such lives as you live do for humanity?'

> *Narrative of Sojourner Truth.*

'I can't read a book, but I can read the people'

> *Narrative of Sojourner Truth.*

List of Sources

'You take no interest in the colored people'

Narrative of Sojourner Truth.

'Instead of sending these people to Liberia,
why can't they have a colony in the West?'

Narrative of Sojourner Truth.

'Lord, what wilt thou have me to do?'

Narrative of Sojourner Truth.

'We have planted the vines,
they have eaten the fruits of them'

Maria W. Stewart, 'An Address,
Delivered at the African Masonic Hall',
Liberator, 27 February 1833.

'The free operatives of Britain manufacture the
material which the slaves have produced'

Sarah Parker Remond, 'The Negroes in the
United States of America', *Journal of Negro
History* 27, no. 2 (April 1942).

'Create something . . . That's the life test at last'

Edmonia Goodelle Highgate, 'Neglected
Opportunities', *Christian Recorder*,
14 July 1866.

List of Sources

*'Often have I been told if I were
a man I would be hung'*

Jennie Carter, 'Letter from Nevada County: Mud
Hill, September 12, 1868', *Elevator*, 25 September 1868.

*'The best way for a man to prove that
he can do a thing is to do it'*

Fannie Jackson Coppin, 'A Plea for Industrial
Opportunity', in *Masterpieces of Negro Eloquence*, ed.
Alice Moore Dunbar (New York:
The Bookery Publishing Company, 1914).

*'We are the heirs of a past which was
not our fathers' moulding'*

Anna Julia Cooper, 'Womanhood a Vital Element in
the Regeneration and Progress of a Race', in her *A
Voice from the South: By a Woman from the South*
(Xenia, Oh.: Aldine Printing House, 1892).

'We are women, American women'

Josephine St Pierre Ruffin,
'Address to the First National Conference
of Colored Women', *The Woman's Era*, 1895.